THOUGHT CATALOG BOOKS

Incompleteness

Incompleteness

AMY DEBELLIS

Thought Catalog Books

Brooklyn, NY

Contents

Part 1

Imago

I have heard it said that as we grow up we become other people.
And that when we die we are miles away from where we began—
In space, time, identity.
We shed the skins of our past selves like insects do,
And with each molting it is easier to look back at one's life
And still keep that enviable cold distance
From things like anger, grief, need.

With each cycle we grow wiser, more contemptuous,
Our self-worth building as old attachments fade.
Lack of change is impossibility. Nothing stays the same.
We draw ourselves hot baths under bright lights
And in them fall asleep and awaken to blackness—
Half-sunk, disoriented, bobbing in freezing water.

A sneaking suspicion has been forming in my mind,
The same mind that has cast off and reconfigured its form
A thousand or more times in my fledgling life.
I have the feeling that someday, each of us will fall asleep
With face upturned towards a lightened sky.
But we will awaken too early, not to growth but to decay:
A dying chrysalis emerging into an endless dark.

Through the Screen

There is lukewarm water pooling in my palms,
Barely clinging to the heat it once held.
Near-senseless, I live in disconnect,
And claw against the muffling dark.
I sense as if through thick paper
The first tinge of autumn on my skin,
Winter's snap approaching on the air—
The burning crackling crisping leaves
I always saw on the ground, but somehow
Never glimpsed in the act of falling.

Is this what it is like to be you?
Living on the other side of a screen.
You evade my touch in much the same way.
You have become a ghost due to the mere fact
Of your existence: face burned into my mind,
While the malformed shadow of you
Skulks around the chambers in my chest.

The further inside you I try to look,
The thicker the barrier becomes.
I have always held more insight
Into others than into myself. But really,
With all that has been said of me—
And all the distance that surrounds—
What can possibly be gleaned
Of the thing that rots inside my heart?

Endings

Love, for us, holds an incompleteness. It's similar
To the way you never manage to reach the last page of a novel
And how I never manage to force out certain words.
You think you know me, but I have my own fantasies, too.
Very different ones from yours. If you tried to speak them
They would catch in your throat like an unknown language.

You see, my fantasies are of leaving. I picture myself
Exiting our house in the cold milky dawn,
Casting your clothes behind me like old shutters,
Abandoning the pages of our book
And leaving them to curl and tear apart in a high wind behind me.
I can hear it now, a roaring like words rushing past my ears.
Words in a language you don't know.

And yet. Some fantasies are only fantasies.
From what I have seen, our leaves won't blow away,
But will instead disintegrate: gradually, undetectable at first,
And then faster as that high wind picks up.
I can't catch hold of the pages—
They slip from my fingers, crumbling,
And I inhale them like dust.

Prayer

I am as a ghost: airless, without voice,
Bones clanking as they fall to dirt
In the rattling dusk. I say: "I am not here."
The shadows on the rocks never answer,
Only fade from black to black—
Murky, shifting like plants under the sea,
Haunted like shrines for old fires.

High tide draws us out again.
Black wind in my hair, black salt on my tongue;
My lips are covered in the darkness of the foam.
I tell the hulking shapes on the sand,
"We are not here."
They never answer, only tremble
As a high wind passes over the huge dark sands.

Monsters

I can't move out of the space I now find myself in.
It's hard to explain in words: chemical sadness, a gray haze.

On my lap, I have a notebook made of leaves.
Creatures multiply in its pages.
I scribbled all these notes in the margins,
Staining ink across the pages alongside spiderweb sketches.
Monstrous shapes: squint and they become nebulous,
Each a tiny Rorschach Test.
I've chronicled my monsters' appearances, their lifespans,
Their dietary and social habits.

You are laughing. You think this is quaint, funny.
But look in front of you: you have your own notebook.
Open it and turn to a picture of me.
You'll find no other creature occupying its pages.
Yes, admit it—you know this of me
As well as I know my own creatures.
I am like a hinge, or a gap, or negative space:
By myself, I do not exist.

Eat the leaves if you are hungry. It's all right, they fit into your diet.
I should know: I sketched you in my notebook, too.
Let me peer over at your notes on me.

Imaginary, does not exist. Fictional creature, perhaps a monster.
Further research possibly necessary.

You are right, as always. I should have known how well you knew me.

Shuffling, tearing, then crackling as we burn the pages.
Smoke rises above us, lingering: this gray haze.

A Darkness

Inside everyone is a thing that they are trying to escape.
Some people run to other countries, other families.
Some seek distraction, white noise—interruption, interference.
Others simply accept their chaos,
Or their anger, or their emptiness.

Some try to cover the thing with love, that ever-redeeming quality
We place so much trust and faith in.
I love you, I love you so much, they say,
Holding their emotion aloft, as though it will illuminate something.

Love helps lessen the darkness, until it becomes the darkness.

Take us, for example. All my feelings for you cancel each other out—

(Warmth fear jealousy hate apathy pity affection)

—everything blurs. All the colors combined form a muddy mess.
Red and blue and gold and green and all those bright brilliant shades
Turn dim and ruined when pushed too close together.
Shapes grow amorphous in a lack of light.

My word for love is darkness.

Incompleteness

Sometimes things slide off the supports they rest on—
(words, ideas, intentions; all of these are things)
—and their underlying truths are revealed:
Reality surging up from below.
Sometimes when I am looking into his eyes I can see it.
Only when we are physically very close,
And something intense on his end is happening—
A logical or intuitive struggle, a quickening of desire—
Can I see it. It's a blankness deep down in the brown.
Not a blackness but a blankness.
Something incomplete.

It's like looking at what you thought was a hole or a well
And suddenly your depth perception rights itself
And you see it is only a black spot on the floor.
Or passing by what you think is a motionless person
But when you glance back, it's really just a mannequin.

In these moments and days and months that pass
I am being held by a mannequin.

If I were to cut myself open, what would spill
Out of the hollows within my body?
Something dark and cloudy, I have been guessing lately.
A cloud that buzzes like a mass of ravenous murderous insects.
A long buzzing that never stops.
What about him?
I feel that deep inside him there are only echoes.
Echoes of the person that could have been,

The man whose shadow he is playing at being.
When he is done playing he will discard that man,
Someone who never existed but almost.

I live from the inside out. Not the other way around.
How, I wonder, does he perceive himself?
I think he exists from the outside in,
Living off of reflections of himself.
Without the mirrors, he would vanish.

Mirrors

I need to write about you. That will make you real.
Flat painted eyes lock onto my startled stare,
Your warm fingers lace with mine, and inches away from you
I can feel the heat that pulses in the hollow of your throat.
When we are caught in between moments,
In the space that separates thought and action,
Intent and understanding,
I can compress all of my feelings into one small word.
That word is not "Love." It is not "Happiness" or "Hope."
It is not even "Snow"— that story that, we thought, described us.
That word is Alone.

I lie next to you at night, at dawn,
Dipping in and out of strange and terrifying dreams,
And feel the steady beat of life next to me.
What makes this real? You will leave me one day,
Or (maybe even perhaps possibly)
I will leave you.
In the end, for all our lives, we will always be separated,
Whether by miles of ocean or a few inches of bedspread,
Or the dizzying walls we erect between us
With my silence and your words.

What makes any of this real?
Whenever I look into your eyes, I can never see anything solid.
They are only two flat mirrors reflecting my own darkness back to me.

Forests

If it were up to me, our story would begin like this:
Me standing there in that drugged, hazy summer,
Grass tickling my feet, my eyes fixed on your back,
As you disappeared into woods already blackening with night.

The words I wanted to call out to you took shape in my mouth
And then solidified, gathered weight, trickled back down my throat.
If I had written it, that story would end with you—
You walking out into that muffling dark.
A hole is nothing but an empty space, you said;
The depths of darkness are only the absence of light.
If one thinks about it properly, it can be velvety, comforting.

So how does one describe the absence of you?
What shape does that take—what color, what quality?
Does it slam down onto us in a rush of wild heated noise?
No. It settles quietly, with finality, like the growth or decline
Of someone you see day after day.

I think of all these things and my heart stutters,
Beats tripping like footsteps down a staircase
Leading into black uncharted waters.

Part 2

Lascaux

Across the world he sees a different moon.
Everything has changed. Inescapable time.
I sit by the window, try to think of things unrelated:
Silk, acorns, tea stains. A field of grass.
These wisps of wind, as smooth as butter.
But despite my efforts it is all linked in some way,
Pulls some common thread in my heart,
Plunges me into a world of my own making
Where everything is him, and he in everything.
A hole in my heart in the shape of his hand.

I get to thinking about places far across the sea.
Stonehenge, Inca ruins, Viking burial grounds,
Vanished Aztec gold. Ghosts in the desert.
The pyramids—even that strikes an echo in me
As I remember lying with him in Argentina,
The Second Coming echoing in my head,
Wondering what rough beast indeed
Was slouching towards Bethlehem to be born.
It turns out it was me. I was the beast.

My mind crawls deeper inside itself, imagining
Places that once existed but no more.
Or at least existed in myth, and what is life
But a myth. History, faded, turns to legend.
I see the hanging gardens, temple of Artemis,
The beacon at Alexandria. The mausoleum.
And then, back to the birthplace of time,

Long before him or me.
My mind wheels out to a place far off
In a cave in what is now France,
(Though then was an untouched wilderness)
Those markings, handprints in the clay:
"I was here."

Manchester

There is no mistaking that voice.
I'm running now, across the moor,
This bleak vast windswept land.
Your voice pulls me and I must come,
Like Jane to her Rochester. I crest a hill
And a mansion rises on the horizon:
Blackened by fire, its dark windows
Hollow like empty sockets.

(Gathering love-sound, you stir me up,
Make me drag my body down the shore
So I can glimpse your sea-shifting face:
Maddening, seductive, fatal.)

I enter and wander through mirrored halls,
Down tilting corridors
That grow narrower before me.
Staircases disappear in my wake;
Half the doors go nowhere,
Emptying onto faceless brick.
Leaves fly around my feet,
Dust and bone-fragments—
But your voice is growing steadily louder.

Finally I find the room
From which all things emanate.
It's deserted, the colors dull and muted
Like a photograph shut for decades in a drawer.
In the center of the floor, a record spins on repeat.

(Vanishing dust-sound, you are like
The memories of tomorrow
And the dreams of yesterday:
Elegiac, directionless, inescapable.)

Avarice

The city streets unfurl beneath me,
Endless: the colors of vanishing bees.
I'm a giant in a child's castle,
An intruder in my own mind.
This flake of mica flashes stardust
And I crush it between my hands.
So you see, I can press the universe
To nothing. I crush ice between my teeth
And burn all my books:
Dead paper curling in the air.
I change the locks on my doors
And put up signs in the windows.
My friends are all faces without names,
Names without faces.
I think I might be, not quite dead,
But not quite alive anymore.
I run my tongue over bruised black teeth.
I haven't smoked for months,
But everything I eat tastes like cigarettes,
Cigars, ashes: a smokeless fire.

13

Maps

From anywhere in your room we could see Cape Town.
Istanbul too, and Turkey, and Greece.
Our gazes skated over the world.
Sometimes your eyes would creep northward to colder territories:
Greenland, Norway, Newfoundland.
That map hung there long after you left for all those places and more:
A lone, silly goose flying south.

Now I linger where we once stood,
Staring at the sprawl of cities and countries,
My eyes catching on Paris and Ibiza and Rome.
I listen to the slowing rain and its gray erasure,
And wonder where you are.
At the very top of the world maybe,
Already swallowed by the white sky,
Where it is never anything but cold.

Severance

These days creep up on me.
I sink to the bottom of my room and to the bottom of my heart,
Fill up like an empty space in the sea.
They are here, as they are always: those kinds of days
When all I want to do is listen to these songs and close my eyes
And wrap myself in the memory of you.
Imagining so hard I can still feel you
(I can still remember the taste)
Around me, inside me. Can still hear your voice,
That strangely gentle coarseness,
Like leather worn smooth.

But I don't get to choose whether it's love I hear in your tone or hatred.
I can't sift through the memories.
They all slip through: water through a sieve.
Once I let one in, the rest are sure to follow.
I get all of you, everything.
Your hatred colors and covers all the things you have ever said.
I don't know what I'm hoping to gain
From this endless treading in water,
These circles I pace around the abandoned,
Drifting islands in my heart.

The Woman

This frantic racing—this trapped feeling.
His words echo nauseating inside my brain.
(It can create problems)
I know he is referring to me.

My mind is the root of it all, the source of all evil.
God created Man, whose first instinct was to sin,
Who brought the first stirrings of evil into Eden
—But it was Woman who really started it, wasn't it?
It was her.

I am Woman and sin is my essence.

(It can create problems)

I am the problem.
I've always been and forever will be the problem.
I imagine he refers to "the woman" with that honorary symbolic title
Because she has cured him; she's healed him
In the wake of the destruction and damage I caused him.

My skin burns, itches to unravel.
I feel like a bug crawling across the surface of the earth.

16

Only

Knowing you're going to die at a certain time,
Everything looks different.
To some people it shrinks the months they have left.
I guess it does to me as well. Makes the slow crawl of time
A little easier to bear.

ONLY

There it is, one of the rare examples
Of a certain phrase that has gotten stuck in my mind forever.
Or in this case, a word. But it feels more like a phrase,
Seems so much longer than just two syllables.
Since I've packed everything into it.

A phrase glimpsed on a train that went, in the end, to nowhere.
It represents the one thing that made my life bearable,
That can still bring me to depths and heights that nothing else can.
That once kept me going after everything else had gone and even

(only)

Now the lack of it means that if I had everything else,
I would still have nothing. Everything and nothing
Is what that word means to me.
And I hold it in my heart. Forever I count down the beats,
Day after after torturous day,
Holding my breath until I can finally stop counting.

17

GWB

The wind unfurls its wings
Against me. I'm shaking,
My life suspended
At the top of the world.

From here I can see the old apartment.
If I squint, I can even see specks on the horizon,
Distant dots: geese flying south
Though it's already the thick of winter.

Just like the times before, I don't really feel
Anything. Just buffeting wind and,
Far below, the wild salt spray of the sea.

I take one last look at the goose on my wrist
And press my mouth to it,
Pretend it's my love.

He will never know.

At long last I release my rusty grip,
Step out into [ ] emptiness

Into the
Rushing rushing blue

(Geese fly south for the winter)

Into the blue

Blue
Blackness.

18

Meeting You at the Café

You can't fool me
With your friendliness, politeness, decorum,
Nor with this carefully maintained space between us.
My body still remembers.
Even now, I see in you what I did a million years ago:
To me you are still love, still safety, still home.
Nine months we've been apart, nine:
Long enough to create a life but not to quench one.
The love that sprang up in my heart
Won't be stilled, it seems.

The only time your words ever made me sick
Was when you told me you wanted me to start over
With someone else.
It would make you happy, you said.
Happy to see me happy.

I think of time and smell salt stirring on the air,
Seagulls circling above me like vultures.
I think of happy—your version of happy—and I sense death.

Part 3

19

Night

I ruined him and he saved me,
Caught me and hauled me up out of my darkening night.
What courage it must have taken him in the midst of his own fears.
Memories spoil just like apples and bodies do.
Everything we are and everything we do—it all goes rotten.
Kisses don't just leave lipstick marks; they etch scars.

Haunted by grief and guilt, insectile, sunk in shame,
I writhe and seek another side of sleep: one without dreams.

But nothing can take me away from here.
Bring me your fastest horses and I'll lay in their path,
Let them trample me, push out my insides.
I don't need them anyway. I am like Eve after Adam died.
I've lost the place I came from, lost my origin,
And there is no compass inside me. My soul is like smoke
And I can't tell whether these lights are signal flares or fireflies.

After a while, though, even that distant glow is gone.
They were just ghosts of stars
Whose deaths haven't yet caught up to them,
But which still remain three hundred million miles ahead of me.
I claw my way through the dark.
I ruined him but he saved me.

20

Passages

Darkness like that at the end of the earth
Beckons from the fourth corridor.
I wait, breath misting fruity on the air,
Imagining how my reflection
Will stretch and distort after midnight.
Like the way you supposedly
Can't read clocks or books in dreams.
But that's false—I read about my own death in a dream once.
I woke not in a panic but with hushed calm,
Relief at the knowledge that I would die, too, eventually.
That great hand in the sky
Never falters. Wish all you want
And there shall be no difference.
It will paint each of our worlds shades forever darker:
Bloodred, bruise-red, then black.

21

Confession

The evening hangs close. I collapse into myself, seeking that
Tenebrous emptiness. My mind unfolds, rolls away.
In between the flickering worlds of dreams, there's a certain frequency
I can't quite catch. Like a radio tuning in and out.

Ten thousand parsecs ahead of me, you float upwards,
Stretching towards the spangled heavens: an exhausting multitude of
stars.
In the end, if you look at it right, art is just a long and languorous
Confession of the soul. Inescapable truth.
Inspect closely enough the things I have written
And you will see everyone I ever was.

If a writer falls in love with you, someone once said, you can never die.

My old gloom, darkly radiant,
Spills out in words I never wanted to release.
You dragged them from me like wild horses, like an army of torturers:
Bright-out, blinding, in the light.

22

Perpetuity

I remember lying half-awake with you in the cool light of dawn.
A lone bird was wheeling in the ashy white sky,
And I remember how my heart was skipping.

But now, a year later, I find it impossible to rest.
The withered autumn and the icy haze
Of oncoming winter are not things by which anyone can live.
I crawl further into myself to escape the outside light.
I feel trapped beneath the endless bowl of the sky.
It sprawls overhead and I am snared in this concrete cell, this building.

Weeks pass and in my head I am building
A new home. A world of my own creation in which I can rest,
Where there are no birds, only a paper sky.
Darkness never comes, just a dreary haze
Bringing with it rain and the kind of light
That makes all things look like they have never been alive.

I haven't paid rent in months, but I doubt that my landlord is still alive.
Steam hisses from the pipes, and there are creaks as my building
Falls a little bit more in on itself each day.
Outside I see a smoky haze gathering.
Winter comes and crushes me beneath its sky.

My memories of faces, things, words…they pass in a sort of haze.
Pieces of the sky detach themselves, float down; with them I am
building
A paper castle. Like a house of cards, in which I can rest

And watch the disintegrating sky. I focus on the cracks, wait for light
To seep through. But there is never any light.

The sky sinks down around me. The old building has vanished.
(Did I get lost in my head?) The light has turned hazy.
I breathe deeply, feel ash catch in my lungs.
And, like a dream,
I am in your bedroom again,
Lying in the cool dawn with you,
Watching that bird wheeling forever in the whiteness.

23

Waste Land

I reach the old crossing-point and unruffle my map.
A nightingale is singing sparks into the wasteland.
The steps we left have already vanished phantomlike into the air,
Oscillating, like me, between real and not-real.
So I carry you forever in silence.

Here we hate the winter but none of us are burdened by snow.
Melting, feathery flakes can't hurt us—
the true danger lies in the winds
That shake these crumbling buildings; the piles of triturated concrete
Frozen above us, hovering on their precipice, ready to fall.

You scooped my love up, gathered it like it had substance. That's why
I am afraid of you.
You sank down into me until you became my skeleton.
Now you're an anterior burden, always present in my mind.
I am haunted by my own nightmares.
I carry you, forever, in silence.

24

Heat Insects

I want to burn away with the sunset, spin the clocks out forever.
I can never advance with the progression of time.
Ahead of me I see no path, no way forwards:
Only a great emptiness, and the shadow of my future self
Creeping forwards into blackness.

Like every other ghost, I hold my secrets.
You—you were the first of them.
I can still smell the dust, glimpse the outline for a blurred moment,
But it vanishes when you look directly at it.
You disappear always, like steam on a winter morning.

I still remember how it was with you: suspended in half-darkness
With Armory lights still slanting through the open window.
Frantic heady rush of night.
I tried to see your face in the gloom, but I couldn't.
I wanted to freeze you like an insect in amber, but I couldn't find you.

I feel this old disease creeping up, bubbling in my body.
The ghosts of everything I've done are swarming like black insects
Over my limbs, erasing them. Turning me un-alive, a being
That does not reflect the light but swallows it.
Negative, perpendicular: the opposite of everything.
Who wants to lie next to a ghost?

Time is not an arrow. All things in this universe
Move from order to chaos. That is the difference
Between past and future. Dream becomes nightmare.

You, too, will grow old and faded in my mind.
Everything falls to ruin in the end: candles burning down.

I pace circles in the gathering night, the summer heat.
If I close my eyes, I can imagine that the insects alighting on my flesh
Are you, come back after all. I let myself let go,
Float in that old ghost-touch, ancient voices:
Relics of love that left a thousand years ago.

25

Like Emotions in the Absence of Language

And you remain entombed in my mind, gone
Like the insects that left their shaky trails
Snaking through the hush our memories planted.

These landscapes aren't what they used to be.
How fitting, that I can only see the beauty in things
Without you. Before, you blocked out
All other wonders, and all I saw was gray haze,
Dead leaves rattling, snow gone ashy with dirt.
But I suppose there's beauty in those things too.
That barren starkness, cold sharp
And unbroken, like something wonderful that happened
Before there was language to describe it.
In the absence of words,
There is nothing left to blur the truth.

I reach back with my tongue, find that
Hollow in my throat, in the space between
Where the sounds ended and the sounds began.
In both the beginning and the end I was always pleading,
Stone words collapsing into silence in my mouth.

26

Deafness

I dreamed I fell in love with you again, but you were deaf.
Instead of saying "I love you," you signed it,
Hands white whispers in the dark.
Even with your face touching mine, you could still read my lips.
Every day, you spelled out wonderful things in the air:
How you treasured me, how you knew I was yours,
How you owned every inch and fiber of my being.
I learned a little sign language, too. You were proud of of me.
We watched movies together at night,
Subtitles flickering on a silent screen.
We were one, our roots entangled and coiled
In the soil of soft salt-earth.

In the same dream, later, you fell in love with a blind girl.
I was the bridge between you two: I translated your signs to language,
and guided her hands so she could trace words on your skin
like a wood-scratching artist discovering paper for the first time.
Her inkstains bloomed like dark flowers, cloudy in the night.

I helped you propose to her. But you never left me.
You took me with you. Every night, the sharp pain of longing
Was dulled, like a stump regrowing after countless amputations;
She slept so deeply that there was no barrier between us.
Afterwards, I would press my lips to your neck,
Laying between the two of you,
Murmuring the same thing she would trace on your skin,
Murmuring
I love you: those flower-words, that dark lingering sound.

About the Author

Amy DeBellis is a writer and fashion student living in Manhattan. Her novella *Penumbra* has also been published by Thought Catalog Books.

Thought Catalog, it's a website.

www.thoughtcatalog.com

Social

facebook.com/thoughtcatalog

twitter.com/thoughtcatalog

tumblr.com/thoughtcatalog

instagram.com/thoughtcatalog

Corporate

www.thought.is

www.ingramcontent.com/pod-product-compliance
Lightning Source LLC
Chambersburg PA
CBHW031633040426
42452CB00007B/800

* 9 7 8 1 9 4 5 7 9 6 2 7 2 *